'WOMEN THE IDLE OF CALMNESS'

WORLD'S PRIDE

ISHITA SAXENA

Copyright © Ishita Saxena
All Rights Reserved.

ISBN 979-888591340-9

This book has been published with all efforts taken to make the material error-free after the consent of the author. However, the author and the publisher do not assume and hereby disclaim any liability to any party for any loss, damage, or disruption caused by errors or omissions, whether such errors or omissions result from negligence, accident, or any other cause.

While every effort has been made to avoid any mistake or omission, this publication is being sold on the condition and understanding that neither the author nor the publishers or printers would be liable in any manner to any person by reason of any mistake or omission in this publication or for any action taken or omitted to be taken or advice rendered or accepted on the basis of this work. For any defect in printing or binding the publishers will be liable only to replace the defective copy by another copy of this work then available.

<u>Copyright</u>

All rights reserved. No part of this publication may be reproduced, stored in or introduced into the retrieval system, or transmitted, in any form, or by any means

(Electronic, mechanical, photocopying, recording or otherwise) without the prior written permission of the publisher. Any person who does any unauthorized act in relation to this publication may be liable to criminal prosecutions and civil claims for damages.

Contents

Acknowledgements

About the book

I decided whenever I would write my first book; I would go for females first. And I did the same. I wrote about the women's situations, difficulties, pain, compromises and a lot of things I agree with. Those who are today's generation have started to understand all these things very well. But somewhere still, it is very important to explain many of these things twice. So this book is all about Women. I hope you all read and like this book.

Thank you!

Preface

ϷϷϷ

The God Decided to Create a Unique World
He picked up the colour brush and used all the colours to decorate
  Some Hills, Some Rivers
  Beautiful flowers Flowing With the Air
  Forests,Birds, Animal &
  A king Without The fear

ϷϷϷ

He gave Reverence, Believes Somewhere
  The Spirit of God was hovering over the waters.
  The Sky, Sea's , Moon & the Shine of Stars
  Dry land , Plants or Shadow of the Trees
  The Heaven, The Earth & The Beautiful Universe
  Finally he made a lot of creatures, Grace & Power
  Colour full Human With the different Dare.
  The heart' , Breaths & The Soul Without Any Colour.
  But something's missing, he said!

ϷϷϷ

Oh! My dear!
  Where is love & Care?
  He was in tension but need to Cover
  Saw here & there
  He saw only Golden colour
  & Made a Lady Figure
  Gave here Some happiness,
  alot of pain & tears
  he was so clear
  That ***WOMEN,THE IDOL OF CALMNESS'*** here!

Then He found Love & Care!

ᗡᗡᗡ

Z

ᗡᗡᗡ

Foreword

ϷϷϷ

So We're talking about

THE WOMEN'

Being a woman is the most difficult ..

Maybe being a woman is a punishment.Questions are raised on everything

If she is a woman, how can she have limitations? What does she not do for loved ones?

She ignores all her happiness, She never even talks about what she likes and what she doesn't! Because your happiness means a lot to her. Your happiness should not be seen by anyone's evil eyes,She never forgets to glance!

She always stops you from going on the wrong path, she does not

think about herself but all of you because she is a woman, she cares.

She does all the things initially for her parents and later on for her family

What does she do for herself ??

Nothing!!!

Because She is Greater than God,Even God worships her.

Although does not know how much pain she endures, yet,she doesn't lose courage & hope!

But there are some limitations here to what extent you bother her or talk with her.

Because just like I said, God also worships her, that is, how can I see her insult and why ??

But it feels very bad thinking that there is a need to tell you about it.

Prologue

History of The Women

In those days her condition was very bad, she did not even have the freedom to say his words.

Rather, nobody wanted to have a daughter.If they had a daughter, he would get upset and abuse her.

She used to learn from the beginning that a woman should only listen to men.

They gave a lot of love to the boys.

The daughters did not even see them properly, to love her was a very big thing then ..

At that time there was a cheap mentality that

They considered the woman like a slaves,

But at that time some such women were born who changed little thinking of them that The Women were only their slaves nothing else..!

"You can tell the condition of a nation by

looking at the status of its Women."

This is a beautiful quote by 'Jawaharlal Nehru' on Women.

Women today are eager to take up professions and work.

So they get respect , Dignity in the family and in their society also. Women in free India also enjoy

equality in work in comparison to men.

Women were very educated but yet suffered from the evils of society . Some open minded people like 'Swami Vivekananda' , ' Iswar Chandra' and others who worked for the well-being of the Women.

ϷϷϷ

Women in India are still exploited and abused.they are still fighting for their rights.

The birth of a female baby is considered a curse in parts of the country which is a very unexpected thing by the human-beings.

Their condition in the village is far worse . Today ,women whom they marry are so dependable and all these things they lose their rights and self - respect. Actually they are not aware yet about all their rights and without any reason fully depend on men.

Thus in our tradition oriented society male dominance still prevails.

Even our Indian women are more intelligent and more hard-working than men. They are full of love, with all these qualities of knowledge and heart . They can do wonders for themselves and for others

In the present day India it is of use to curse and bemoan their fate as the weaker sex.

They should raise their voice against injustice, unwanted behaviour, abuse, ill-treatment. The future of women in India seems bright but it is women themselves who can ensure it by being vigilantly alert United. It is said that God helps those who help themselves and it equally applies in the case of the rights and Liberty of Women in India.

However, ending against women is still a challenge. We can prevent ills by ensuring women autonomy and also increase participation and decision making power in the family and public life both.

ᐅᐅᐅ

She said

WE ARE The SAME!

We are the same.
    I & You are human beings;
    We are living in the same Circle ring;
    But, There is many Different things.
    Not by the face
    Not by the race;
    Is all about the matter of Your thinking Place.
    All of us Are like to the rays;
    Our father God is one & The same Always
    In the Temple, The Guru dwara, The Masjid We all go For making
Prayers.
    We are the Same ;
    The Sun gives the power to all with same raise;
    The moon shows it's light with the same dress;
    The Air Touches our body with the same ways;
    There is no alien , No difference in the vales;
    She Said; We are the Same no matter Who believes!

ᐅᐅᐅ

Why Do Women Cry ??

One day the Woman was crying all day. His son asked her, "Why
are you crying?" She hugged him and told him because I'm a
woman.

The little boy doesn't understand his mother's words .

Next morning the boy asked his Father,"Why does mother seem to
cry for no reason?"

"All Women do cry for no reason."

Was all his Father could say and give him a big smile about this
question.

The little boy grew up and became a man ,but still wants to find the
Answer of his question, " Why do Women cry."

Finally he put in a call to God,when God got on the Phone ,He asked
"God why do women cry so easily?"

God said,

"When I made the Women she had to be special'.

I made her Shoulder strong enough to carry the weight of the world
yet gentle enough to give comfort.

I gave her inner power to endure childbirth and the rejections that
many times comes from her children

I gave her a hardness that allows her to keep going when everyone
else gives up and takes care of her family through sickness and fatigue
without complaining.

I gave her the sensitivity to love her children any and all
circumstance , even when her child has hurt her very badly

I gave her faith in herself to carry her husband through his faults
and fashioned her from his rib to protect his heart.

And finally , I gave her tears to shed , this is her's exclusively to use
when

It's needed."

God said , "You see my son,

The beauty of a woman is not in the dress she wears, not in the figure
that she carries .

The beauty of a woman must be seen in her eyes because that is the
doorway to her heart - the place where love and care resides."

Now he understood that God has made The Women' so strong that she is do cry

but never gives up in any situation

He used to respect Women a lot before and now he started doing more.

ᗧᗧᗧ

Here, women also need to understand that they are

Made by God for Special dares, not for those who don't know how to give respect to The Women.

Women should raise their voice against any crime ..

If she hears anything from anyone once, she will always listen. If she finds something wrong, she should tell it from the beginning .

You are not weak , you are the strongest person in this world .

She has a lot of power to bear anyone's unexpected unwanted words . But no need to bear

anything without any reason , because ; "You all are special." The God Said .

There is nothing that She' can't handle!

She has been suffering from pain that couldn't not be handled by the man

She has been heartbroken

She has been defeated

She complete her dreams in dreams

She can do a lot, she has a lot of skepticism But,

She felt very down ,When she did not consider her anything.

Yet she always finds the right way to.

To lift herself up again .

She is fighter

She is courageous

She is beautiful

She is unbreakable

She is You!

There are a lot of examples of Women that do everything even if they do all the things which can't be done by the Man.

In front of whom the King Maharajas bowed their heads and they were proud of them.

You must have known all about Rani Maha Laxmi Bai, she gave her life but did not bow her head in front of British and that British liked it so much.

He wrote a book & showed the courage of Rani Maha Laxmi Bai!

ᗡᗡᗡ

BARKHA DUTT

Fearless is a synonym for 'Barkha Dutt'. The intrepid television journalist ,most famously known for her reporting during the Kargil War' between India and Pakistan, 1999. Emblematic figure of , New Delhi , Television limited , better known as ND T.v , Barkha Dutt' was one of the most prominent face's of news channel for 21 years , She has been a face of in Spiration for countless young girls & Women who courageously embraced field of hardcore journalism.

ᗡᗡᗡ

Irom Chanu Sharmila

Known as the 'Iron Lady'. Irom Chanu Sharmila has been a symbol of undeterred will. A Civil Rights and Political activist.She went on a hunger strike lasting 16 years , Protesting against forces special powers act ordained by the Indian armed forces unregulated power of action . Due to the misuse of power by the army , which vowed to renounce food & Water in what led to the longest hunger strike in the world.

ᗏᗏᗏ

<u>Sojourner Truth</u> *(1797 – 1883)*

"Truth is powerful and it prevails."

Sojourner Truth is one of the most inspirational black women in America's history and her words belong to one of the most famous speeches by any woman. An African-American abolitionist and women's rights activist, Truth delivered a now famous speech at the Ohio Women's Tights Convention in Akron, 1851, that has come to be known as "Ain't I a Woman?"

Truth was separated from her family at the age of nine and was subsequently sold for auction as a slave along with a flock of sheep *for $100. In 1829, Truth escaped to freedom with her infant daughter Sophia, but her other two children had to be left behind.*

Truth began to advocate for the rights of women and African Americans in the late 1840's and was known for giving passionate speeches about women's rights, prison reform and universal suffrage. Truth, who died in Michigan in 1883, is known as one of the foremost leaders of the abolition movement and one of the earliest advocates for women's rights.

Sonika Gahlot Founder of - Happieesouls

Happieesouls motto and the aim is to create a sustainable Lifestyle as a culture across India.This was the biggest dream for Sonika Gahlot. when she was mature also said to her mother .That she wants to do something different for India. She felt very proud after listening to her daughter's dream and always appreciated her .

Most of the time Their contact never worked, sometimes certain NGO's didn't even exist physically when she visited there for want to tell her plan . Then the idea surprised her, that's when the idea of 'HappieeSouls' was born .

Speaking to 'LifeBeyondNumbers' Sonika looks back at how it all started and the kind of impactHappieesouls is making, sharing the challenge and the road ahead . Happieesouls picks up these unused , unwanted goods and delivers them directly to the NGO of your choice.

The customers also get real-time updates, and confirmation of delivery to their NGO's .

"We bring structure to the donation of old unwanted household items. The current market is very unorganized , where clothing and non-clothing items get dumped into donation boxes in societies or corporate houses and then later require a tremendous amount of time, energy and resources to segregate and send the clothing to the needy.", Stated Sonika.

Everyday they are partnering with NGOs and enterprises who are also into upcycling and work for the upliftment of underprivileged Women.

And overall extremely positive feedback from all the NGOs and customers says Sonika. To date HappieeSouls has enabled over 700 customers to donate over 15,000 pieces of masks, apparels, stationary and a variety of other supplies.

ᗡᗡᗡ

It wants to say to the Women don't be a lady like society wants , be the lady that you want.

These Women of Steals have inspired me to be Brave and never let anyone or anything stop me from being the best version to myself.

I salute their undying spirit

ᗡᗡᗡ

Women are the real spirit of CALMNESS‘

Someone says "When you educate a man you educate only a man but, if you educate a woman you educate a whole generation".

All of you tell everyone there is full freedom in our country,but do you ever think that a lady, a girl or a woman can walk alone at night ??

Can they choose Their future ??

Can they open their words in front of men??

No, they don't then how can society say that there is full freedom in their country.?

I definitely accept that men also have pain and they have also stressed to earn money for their family .

But they have rights to get rid of their anger

They can vent their anger on women.

We bear everything Everyday without saying a couple of words.

We don't have that , that's why

we're asking?

We never told you to treat us like a God, we just want the respect that we deserve.

Theshoulder of a man can bear the burden of the body only,

But , a

Woman carries the burden of a Soul .

Whether this world has survived or doesn't exist without a man , the absence of a Woman will end the World'.

ᕔᕔᕔ

She is great

Tears in her heart and still laugh from outside

Gets her hair scattered over and over again.

Because she feels not good

Everything gets left behind as soon as she gets married .

Her childhood is left to her friends, her freedom.

She cover the torn ankles with her Sari

Take care of her family more than herself.

She is the most afraid of everyone accumulating her authority.

When a girl goes to her in laws house after getting married

She leaves her maternal house

And She change all the customs, She change her choices

She change her dreams

She changed herself.

When she comes into the house the courtyard are filled with happiness, feeds the whole family and then she eats herself

If a woman takes care of her life then Everyone's life is taken care of.

How much has the daughter changed after marriage??

Afterall why would a woman speak fearfully

in the voice of Slavery?

Wake-up in Slavery?

Sleeps in Slavery?

Murders caused by dowry

She died in her four walls.

The day she learn to raise her voice will find her dream home on that day change herself society will change

That day will also come when the whole in law will sit and eat food with her but freedom also means you don't forget

Freedom is equality not governance.

The woman of the orthodox household is still a slave it works like a machine all day long from Mountain of sorrows it falls like a waterfall Because She is great.

ᐅᐅᐅ

Yes ! I'm proud to be a Woman..!

Break every cage
      Know when I'll fly
      Regardless of what you
      Want to do, still the
      Distant sky I'll make my place
      Yes! I'm Proud to being a Woman'
      Even though the people of the world have tied my feet with the
traditional chain.
      Break the chains ,I'll show the world to Noone less than anyone
      Yes! I'm Proud to be a Woman'.
      Their house had nothing in my name. The light of the day went into
      Making the dreams The sleeps of the night Passed away to put the
children to sleep
      The house where nothing' in my Name All my life was spent
decorating that house.

ᐅᐅᐅ

<u>A Story of A Woman...</u>

Woman is the form of Annapurna, so if needed, she can also take the form of Durga and Kali. The woman keeps on becoming a victim of domestic violence many times to save the family, but once she decides to get out of this bondage, then she becomes an example for others. Priyanka Singh is sharing with you the story of some such women who have found a place in the face of domestic violence.

She was from a noble family of Kolkata. Never had seen any kind of problem in life but after marriage everything changed. Both my husband and mother-in-law had a very bad attitude towards me. He got me fired. They used to demand dowry continuously. When the demand was not met, I started beating. I got married in 1992 and a year later my daughter was born. During pregnancy, my husband pushed me down the stairs.

With great difficulty, my and my daughter's life were saved.

The daughter was about 3 years old, so fed up with the beatings of her husband and mother-in-law, I went to my parents and told them everything but the father and brother refused to give any help. Mother could not help me even after wanting. I had to return to my husband. Now the atrocities of those people increased further. Maybe they thought no one would help me. Due to the assault, I had to stay on the bed for about 8 months during this time. The second time a son was born but the atrocities of those people continued. Even for the children, the husband did not pay the expenses. Then I started writing free-lancing. However, the husband would constantly doubt and beat me about money. My son was affected by the assault, and by the time he was 5 years old, he became silent and almost forgot to speak. Despite being normal, he had to put up with children with learning disabilities. That's it, that was the moment when I felt that now there is no option but to get out of this marriage!

After suffering atrocities for 10 years, she left her husband and his house at the age of 35 and came to Delhi. When she requested her parents, they let her stay in their Delhi flat. In the initial phase, she spent some money by selling her jewellery. Then slowly started free-lancing in the advertising world, started writing. Gradually she joined the 'Crime Against Women Cell' of Delhi Police and started counseling women victims of domestic violence there for free. She worked here from 2009 to 2013.

In 2010, I was featured in the Delhi Police's 'Crime Against Women Cell' calendar. Till now she has got 13 books in total. She has counseled thousands of women. She is invited to lecture on gender sensitivity in schools and colleges. Corporate companies take my opinion on sexual harassment issues. Her Trust also provides free legal advice to women victims of domestic violence and legal aid to women earning less than 5000.

When there was domestic violence with me, She used to constantly ask God; "Why all this happened to me?" Today She has found the answer to that 'why'. She probably had to do so many things, help others, so maybe God made her go through that torture. The real victory lies in getting out of sorrow and finding moments of happiness for yourself and others. After doing English Honors from St. Stephen's College, she went to England on scholarship and at the age of just 25 is working as a consultant in the Ministry of Women and Child Development.

Son is also pursuing an MA in Gender Studies. She got many awards like Nari Shakti Award, Karmaveer Jyoti Award, Neerja Bhanot Award, First Women Award but She feels that her real award is her children, because of which she got the purpose of living and She was able to reach here.

ᑭᑭᑭ

Actually !!!

Human life cannot be imagined without women.

it would be called madness to ignore their talents only on the logic that they are less powerful and less virtuous than men. Women represent almost half of the population of India. If their potential is not taken care of, then it clearly means that half of the population of the country will remain uneducated and if women are not educated than that country will never be able to progress.

We have to understand that if a woman, being illiterate, manages the house so well, then how well

an educated woman will handle the society and the country .

Women make the family, the family makes the house, the home makes the society and the society makes the country. It simply means that the contribution of women is everywhere. It is futile to imagine society ignoring the potential of women. Without education and women empowerment, development of family, society and country cannot take place. A woman knows when and how to deal with troubles. If need be, just to give freedom to his dreams.

ᑭᑭᑭ

What the author meant to say is this....
Respect them. She takes a lot of pain and doesn't even let you feel it.

ᗑᗑᗑ

CELEBRATE...

Get in the habit of celebrating
The women that support you
The ones Who lift you up always when you feel low.
Who share love & adjust each other crown ,
The love that mother has is unique
&
So rare
No matter how you hurt her
It'll just never fade it!

ᗑᗑᗑ

About the Author:

THIS IS ISHITA SAXENA, BELONGS TO BAREILLY, UTTAR PRADESH, HER AGE IS 19 YEARS, SHE DOING HER STUDIES FOR BCOM FINAL YEAR. SHE IS FOND OF WRITING SINCE CHILDHOOD BUT SHE STARTED WRITING HER WORDS IN BOOKS AS A CO-AUTHOR 2

YEARS AGO. SHE MOSTLY LIKES TO WRITE ABOUT LIFE. BY THE WAY, SHE HAS JUST WRITTEN HER WORDS IN A LOT OF BOOKS, AS A CO-AUTHOR APART FROM THIS SHE HAS ALSO PRESENTED HER WORDS IN MAGAZINES. AND RECENTLY SHE OPENED HER OWN WRITING COMMUNITY NAMED - 'ADMIRE OF ILLUSION ' This is the very first book she wrote.

ᗑᗑᗑ

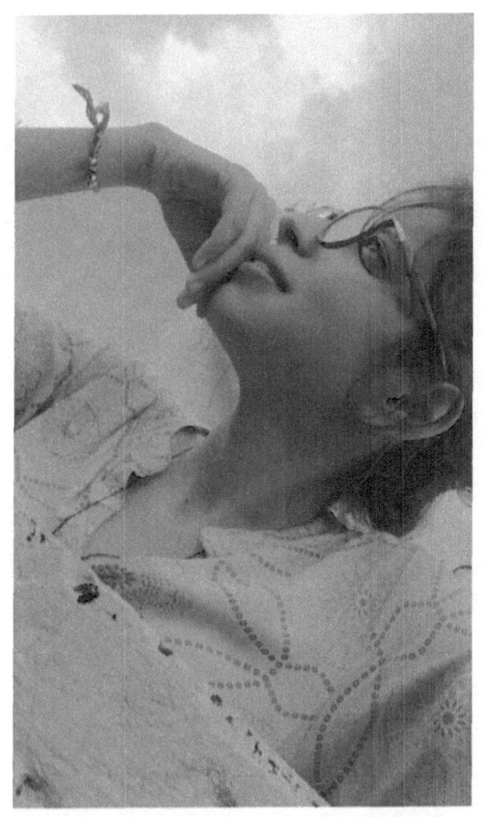

ISHITA SAXENA(AUTHOR)

$\heartsuit\heartsuit\heartsuit$

Dear Women

You are the only one in front of whom everyone is weak ..
GOD made you and you made us
According to me you are not less than God ..
You take a lot of pain in your life
But
Still, how much do you take care of everyone ..
You think about everyone much before You think about Yourself..
You are very strong,
Very beautiful,
You have a lot of courage
You are very tolerant.
There is no one like you ...
You are the Best
You are Divine
You are Actually a Miracle lady...!

$\heartsuit\heartsuit\heartsuit$

-Thanks for Reading-

www.ingramcontent.com/pod-product-compliance
Lightning Source LLC
Chambersburg PA
CBHW020947160726
47993CB00007B/2978